IMPORTANT NOTICE

Do not use this book until you have read these pages.

You have in your hands one half of the system that will change your life. To achieve success it is essential that you download the other half of this system from the Hay House website:

hayhouse.com/mckenna

and use the audio session that completes it.

This is not just a book to read, it is part of a life-changing solution. This book is the first essential element of the system. The audio session is just as important: you must use both the book and the audio session to achieve permanent success.

The session contains everything I would do if I were working with you personally. It includes simple, powerful psychological techniques and a hypnotic trance that strengthen the power of your subconscious mind to guide your success.

The session is really easy to download onto your computer or smartphone, just a few clicks, then a few minutes later, you will have me there whenever you need, to help you make the changes you want.

Intellectual knowledge is not the same as real change, so you cannot expect lasting results if you only read this book. You must download and use the psychological techniques and guided hypnosis to achieve permanent, positive change.

In hypnotic trance your unconscious is highly receptive to positive intentions. It is not the same as sleep, it is a wonderful state of deep relaxation, like a daydream or meditation, and even though you are deeply relaxed, if for any reason you need to awaken, you will do so with all the resources you need.

The audio techniques are not just essential, they are also enjoyable and rewarding. In fact, many people use them over and over to reinforce their new mind-set and enhance their success.

Ensure your success now. Go online now to:

hayhouse.com/mckenna

1. Input the product ID and download code shown below (also found on the card at the front of this book) and then download the free session right now:

Product ID: 5317

Download code: mckenna

2. Regularly use the session as directed in this book.

3. Enjoy it and relax, knowing you are now on your way to lasting success!

CONTROL STRESS

Stop Worrying and Feel Good Now!

WITHDRAWN

PAUL MCKENNA, PH.D.

EDITED BY MICHAEL NEILL

HAY HOUSE, INC.
Carlsbad, California • New York City
London • Sydney • Johannesburg
Vancouver • New Delhi

Published and distributed in the United States by: Hay House, Inc.:
www.hayhouse.com® • *Published and distributed in Australia by:* Hay
House Australia Pty. Ltd.: www.hayhouse.com.au • *Published and distributed in the United Kingdom by:* Hay House UK, Ltd.: www.hayhouse
.co.uk • *Published and distributed in the Republic of South Africa by:*
Hay House SA (Pty), Ltd.: www.hayhouse.co.za • *Distributed in Canada
by:* Raincoast Books: www.raincoast.com • *Published in India by:* Hay
House Publishers India: www.hayhouse.co.in

Cover design: Alex Tuppen

Previously published in Great Britain in 2009 by Bantam Press, an imprint of Transworld Publishers, ISBN: 9780593056295.

Library of Congress Cataloging-in-Publication Data

Names: McKenna, Paul, 1963- author. | Neill, Michael, editor Title: Control stress : stop worrying and feel good now! / Paul McKenna,
  Ph.D. ; edited by Michael Neill.
Description: Carlsbad, California : Hay House, Inc., [2017]
Identifiers: LCCN 2017013532 | ISBN 9781401949136 (paperback)
Subjects: LCSH: Stress management. | BISAC: SELF-HELP / Stress Management. |
  SELF-HELP / Self-Hypnosis. | SELF-HELP / Personal Growth / General.
Classification: LCC RA785 .M35 2017 | DDC 155.9/042--dc23 LC record
available at https://lccn.loc.gov/2017013532

Tradepaper ISBN: 978-1-4019-4913-6

10 9 8 7 6 5 4 3 2 1
1st edition, August 2017

Printed in the United States of America

Thanks to
Gillian Blease, Dr. Keith Blevens, Kate Davey,
Dr. Robert Holden, Natheera Indrasenan, Robert Kirby,
Mari Roberts, Clare Staples, Alex Tuppen,
Dr. Hugh Willbourn, and Doug Young

A QUICK WORD FROM PAUL MCKENNA

Congratulations—you are about to have a healthier, happier life!

The research is astounding—as a result of having greater control over the stress in your life, you will feel better and live longer. Your immune system will be stronger, your stamina will be significantly increased, and you will make better decisions. Better still, the overall quality of your life will be significantly enhanced!

Everybody has some stress, but hardly anyone has the skills to deal with it. An astonishing 50 percent of the reasons why people go the doctor are stress related, and one recent scientific study showed that in the current economic climate, more people are missing work from stress-related problems than ever before.

The techniques in this book are a distillation of what many of the world's leading doctors are saying will improve your health and many of the world's business leaders say will increase your efficiency and effectiveness in the workplace.

But this book isn't just for people who are stressed out about life or who worry too much. It is for anyone who wants to be more relaxed, more resilient, and feel a whole new level of real joy!

More than just a book, this is a *stress control system*, and at its heart is a powerful hypnotic trance that will help you to achieve deep states of relaxation, have more energy, and be more effective in your everyday life.

Many scientific studies have shown that hypnosis is one of the fastest-acting and long-lasting solutions for stress-related illness, and I have packed over twenty-five years of research and months of careful scripting to create a daily companion for you that will allow you to access your body's natural capacity for instant calm and deep relaxation. As you learn to change your response to stress and worry, you will be able to stay at your best for longer and bounce back quicker than ever before.

Interestingly when people attend my hypnosis workshops, they often report that not only do they feel better, the people who know them well tell them they actually look younger.

This comes as no surprise to me. When I first see a client with a stress-related problem, it's usually etched in the tension on their faces. When we're done, they look completely different—unburdened and relieved of the stress they have been carrying around with them wherever they go. And this is what I want for you—a happy, calmer, rich and joyous life!

Living on the Edge

Some people say to me that they need their stress because they worry that without it, they would lose their edge. Every part of this system has been thoroughly tested on some of the highest achievers in the world, and I can assure you that it will in no way take away from your overall abilities.

In fact, as you learn to control your stress, eliminate unnecessary worry, and relax in the midst of your daily life, you will have more energy, become *more* efficient, *more* effective, and your levels of happiness will go through the roof. The ability to have just the right amount of relaxed alertness to deal with any difficult situation is the key to mastering stress and worry, and it is the core skill that you will develop as you use the techniques in this book.

You will still have a full dynamic range of emotions, able to get angry or sad and respond appropriately to any situation. But the overall landscape of your emotions will change. You will experience less anger, less fear, less physical discomfort and a greater sense of background happiness and well-being.

How to Use This System

There are two parts to the system—the book and the hypnotic trance.

You will notice that the book is made up of a series of short chapters. Each chapter will take you no more than ten minutes to read, and contains important information that will deepen your understanding of how your mind and body really work.

Most chapters also contain one or two techniques for you to practice. All you need to do is follow my instructions and these techniques will prepare your body and mind for any situation you may find yourself in, no matter how stressful or worrying it may seem.

While you might be tempted to read through the entire book in one sitting, when it comes to relaxation, faster isn't better—it's just faster! If you like, carry the book around with you and do each exercise as many times as you need to experience its full effect.

To give yourself a rock-solid foundation for your ongoing sense of calm, relaxation, and well-being, use the hypnotic trance each day to go as deeply into trance as you need. Each time you go into trance, the effect becomes stronger, and you reinforce all the positive changes you are making at the unconscious level.

Use it every day for a week and you'll find that as your relaxed alertness increases and your stress diminishes, your enjoyment of life increases and your health will improve too.

I have created this book and hypnotic trance to be an oasis of peace in a stress-filled world—a quick time-out that will allow you to live more fully in each and every moment of your life!

To your health, success, well-being, and joy,

Paul McKenna

THE INSTANT CALM
HYPNOTIC TRANCE

Your mind is like a computer—it has its own software that helps you to organize your thinking and behavior. Having worked with all sorts of people with different problems over many years, I have learned that almost all problems stem from the same cause—negative programs running in the unconscious mind.

This book comes with a powerful hypnotic trance that will fill your unconscious mind with positive thoughts and feelings (you can find the details on the special card at the front of the book). While you become absorbed into a natural state of deep relaxation, I will reprogram your unconscious mind to eliminate unnecessary worry and feel good.

Each time you listen, it will become easier to relax and the positive programming will go deeper into your mind. The latest research into the effectiveness of these and similar techniques has shown that repeated listening to this hypnotic trance will dramatically enhance your ability to control your stress and relax deeply.

You don't have to believe it—just use it!

CHAPTER ONE

•

All You Need to Know about Stress

Background Stress

> *"If you ask what is the single most important key to longevity, I would have to say it is avoiding worry, stress and tension. And if you didn't ask me, I'd still have to say it."*
>
> GEORGE BURNS

I have been working as a therapist for over 20 years with all kinds of people who have all kinds of problems. And if I could help people make only one change, it would be to give them the ability to control their stress and to relax whenever and wherever they want to. This would not only make them feel better, it would lead to changes on every level and in every area of their lives.

When people try to push ahead to get things done when their minds are filled with worry and their bodies are filled with stress, their performance, relationships, and enjoyment all tend to suffer. It is like trying to run a race in a suit of armor—it can be done, but nowhere near as well or even as quickly as if you stopped to take the armor off first.

Yet for many people, they have been so stressed for so long that they have become used to it. They don't even realize how much better life can be. Often it takes some kind of wake-up call, like a relationship breakup, the loss of a job, or a physical illness to make them aware that something is wrong.

Psychologists call the cumulative effects of adapting to more and more uncomfortable circumstances "background stress," and chances are that unless you are already highly practiced at relaxing deeply, you are experiencing it right now.

It often goes unnoticed in the body for a long while, but can surface in the form of bad moods, loss of a sense of humor, headaches, bumping into things, making silly mistakes, and ultimately even depression, anxiety, and physical illness.

Ironically, it is often only when they first begin to relax that people begin to notice the tension that was there all the time.

Understanding the Stress Response

While I will explain a bit about the science of stress and relaxation a little later in the chapter, a simple way to think about it is that our body's stress response works like a car alarm. It is designed to keep us safe by alerting us to the presence of danger in our immediate environment.

But instead of alerting us with a loud and annoying sound, our internal alarm system lets us know that something is wrong by creating changes in our neurochemistry. If you've ever experienced knots in your stomach, periods of excessive anger, fear, or irritation, inability to focus, or even insomnia, chances are your body was paying the price in those moments for the brain chemistry of stress.

So if it's so uncomfortable, why not just eliminate stress altogether?

This is not only impractical, it would be dangerous. Let's go back to the metaphor of the car alarm. If the alarm is switched off altogether, the car is exposed to continual danger without there being any way of your knowing about it until it is too late.

It would be like walking through the jungle without any fear signal in the presence of a poisonous snake or predatory animals—while it might feel "nice" to be so relaxed, your body actually *needs* the stress response not only to alert you to danger but also to pump extra adrenaline into your heart and extra blood and oxygen to your arms and legs.

However, if the car alarm goes off any time someone just looks at the car with a bit of an attitude, it becomes equally useless. Not only do we stop paying attention to it, it begins to drive us and everyone around us a little bit crazy. In the case of our bodies, walking around in a constant state of alarm also has some pretty alarming health consequences, something we will explore in greater depth in the next chapter.

That's why one of the main goals of our time together is the resetting of your internal stress mechanism to a healthy, useful, and appropriate level of sensitivity. We will be doing this in two main ways:

1. Learning to reinterpret the causes of your stress.

2. Learning to reactivate your body's natural stress-reduction system.

As you read through this book, do the exercises, and listen to the hypnotic trance each day, your internal stress mechanism will begin to reset. You will continue to be safe and alert, and will only experience your stress response when your internal protection system is trying to let you know that there is something to pay attention to.

Everyone's daily life naturally has some stress in it, and we have a natural method of relieving that stress within us. Unfortunately, for many of us, the pace of modern life has led us to ignore our own natural stress control. I'm now going to explain how your natural stress control system works and show you how to reactivate it.

Balancing Out the Stress Response

Our bodies are truly miraculous. Without your even having to pay attention, your autonomic nervous system (ANS) keeps your heart beating, your lungs breathing, and ensures that just the right amount of blood and oxygen is pumped through your system to keep everything functioning optimally.

In order to provide balance, the ANS is made up of multiple parts. The most important of these in understanding and beginning to control your stress are the *sympathetic* nervous system (SNS) and the *parasympathetic* nervous system (PNS).

Imagine yourself going for a walk in the park on a nice, sunny day. Suddenly, a mad dog appears around the corner and is coming straight for you. Do you turn and run away or stay to defend yourself?

The SNS governs the "fight or flight" response, flooding your system with adrenaline and cortisol and pumping extra blood and oxygen to your limbs so that you can run away more quickly or fight with more strength.

If you've ever wondered how the stories of mothers lifting cars off their children to save their lives could possibly have happened, the SNS is the answer, and as such plays an incredibly important role in your body's defense. However, left unchecked, all that extra adrenaline and cortisol will take its toll on your system.

So while the SNS is doing its best to help you prepare for fight or flight, the parasympathetic nervous system (PNS) is there to help you to "rest and digest."

Imagine the same scenario as before. You are walking in the park on a nice, sunny day. There are no dogs anywhere and just the right amount of people. You sit down to relax under a tree and your body begins to recharge—your heart beats more slowly, which in turn decreases your blood pressure and whatever food is in your system begins to be digested.

This is your body's natural impulse to rest, relax, and recuperate, and is technically known as the "parasympathetic response." However, since the parasympathetic response is a part of your body's natural design, I will be referring to it as *natural relaxation*.

Natural relaxation is the sweet, soft feeling you get in your muscles when you have finished some heavy work or vigorous movement. You also feel a natural high caused by the release of endorphins, the body's natural opiates.

Now, wonderful though that may feel, it would be virtually impossible to function if that's how you felt all the time. So both systems work together to keep you functioning perfectly.

In an ideal world, we would spend the majority of our time going in and out of a feeling of relaxed alertness. When we wanted to relax deeply, say before drifting off to sleep at night, we could do so quickly and easily. But if the situation called for it, we would get an immediate burst of "stress chemicals" to enable us to respond appropriately to a potentially dangerous situation.

What we think of as "being stressed" is simply the result of one system (the stress response) doing too much and the other system (natural relaxation) not being used enough.

So what triggers the stress response? And how can we begin to control it and in so doing regain control over our busy lives?

The answers to these questions and more will unfold over the next few chapters . . .

CHAPTER TWO

•

The Master Key
to Controlling Stress

The Power of Negative Thinking

> *"There is more to life than increasing its speed."*
>
> Mohandas K. Gandhi

Any average day in life has its demands and stresses—driving to work there's a traffic jam, you get into an argument, you receive an unexpected bill, the kids have made a mess or you are criticized.

These things may not seem like "threats" to you consciously, but your nervous system does not differentiate between a physical threat to your body and a mental or emotional threat to your ego. So if someone criticizes you, your mind responds to the situation with a stress response that produces adrenaline and cortisol in your bloodstream—the same stress chemicals that would be produced if you were under physical attack.

The father of modern stress research, Dr. Hans Selye, summed up this idea in one simple sentence:

"It is not the event, but rather our interpretation of it, that causes our emotional reaction."

This is why you don't need to change the world, your job, your relationships or even your financial situation in order to begin controlling your stress. As your perception and interpretation of an event changes, the intensity and duration of the stress response will change with it.

You will naturally begin to interpret your experiences differently and begin to respond more effectively to the events in your life. Then, you can set about changing whatever needs to be changed on the outside from a place of relaxed alertness on the inside.

As we've already explored, the stress response originally evolved as something practical—a way for our ancestors to get a burst of energy and strength that would enable them to fight a wild animal or run away.

But in today's fast-paced society, the attacks our nervous system is protecting us from are largely imaginary. If you stop for a moment and think about something you have been stressed about, chances are that there is no real physical danger involved—just discomfort.

So we are continually preparing ourselves to deal with physical emergencies that never happen. Many people are in effect responding too often to "the power of negative thinking." And what's interesting is that the human nervous system cannot tell the difference between a real and a vividly imagined event.

This means that even when you just *imagine* looking bad or suffering some threat to your ego, you are producing the very same stress chemicals your body needs to fight or flee. While these chemicals would be useful in the case of an actual, physical emergency, they are meant to be used up and eliminated through physical activity.

The problem comes when those chemicals are released into your system in response to thoughts *that you can neither fight nor run away from*. Because your body has no way to just get rid of them, over time the buildup of those stress chemicals becomes toxic, and can cause all manner of illness and disease.

What can we conclude from all this?

**That the major threat to our health in
modern life is no longer outside us.**

It is the threat of being attacked by our own built-in defense system—the body's stress response. Fortunately, there is a simple solution. As you learn to control your stress and boost your natural levels of relaxation, your health and well-being will increase almost immediately . . .

Discovering the On/Off switch for Natural Relaxation

Almost 20 years ago, research in the field of neurocardiology introduced the idea of a functional *heart-brain*. They discovered that the human heart has its own nervous system inside it that is so sophisticated it functions almost like a second brain.

This heart-brain has at least 40,000 neurons—as many as are found in various subsections of the brain. In fact, it has such elaborate neurological circuitry that it is actually capable of learning, remembering, feeling and sensing things independent of the brain in the head.

Every time your heart beats, it is sending information to the head-brain that influences our perceptions, emotions, and awareness, as well as having a regulatory influence on many of the ANS signals—including the stress response.

What this means is that the human heart is not just a pump for blood—it is the physical control center that determines whether to trigger the sympathetic or parasympathetic nervous system—the stress response or natural relaxation.

Here's how it works:

1. Your head-brain takes in information through the five senses and then re-presents that information in the form of internal language and imagery.

2. If it perceives a threat, real or imagined, it sends a signal down to the heart to produce adrenaline, cortisol, and other chemicals that will increase the body's alertness and its ability to fight off or run away from that threat.

3. However, the *heart-brain can override that signal*. It's like having a remote control "off switch" for our car alarm.

The Institute of Heartmath was set up in the early 1990s to further study the role of the physical heart in health and well-being. Their work and its applications have become so successful that their stress-management programs have been taken up around the world, including by all the branches of the U.S. military.

What they discovered was that actively focusing on the physical heart measurably reduced the presence of stress hormones, increased DHEA, and other anti-aging hormone levels, and enabled peak performance in a variety of situations.

While they have developed a number of tools for increasing the coherence between the electromagnetic signals of the heart-brain and the head-brain, they are all built around one basic idea—that when you shift your attention from your head to your heart, your body relaxes, your mind gets clearer, and your brain releases the positive chemical changes of natural relaxation . . .

FROM HEAD TO HEART

You can use this exercise any time you are experiencing a stressful feeling in your body or an overly busy mind. It will help you to feel better almost immediately—usually in less than a minute. In addition, you may get insights into actions you can take to make things more the way you want them . . .

1. Become aware that you are experiencing a stressful feeling in your body or that your mind is racing.

2. Put your hand on your heart and focus your energy into this area. Take at least three slow and gentle breaths into your heart, maintaining your focus on the feeling of your hand in the center of your chest.

3. Now, recall a time when you felt really, really good—a time you felt love, joy, or real happiness! Return to that memory as if you are back there again right now. See what you saw, hear what you heard, and feel how good you felt.

4. As you feel this good feeling in your body, imagine your heart could speak to you. Ask your heart how you could take better care of yourself in this moment and in this situation.

5. Listen to what your heart says in answer to your question and act on it as soon as you can.

The more you practice this exercise, the easier it becomes to interrupt the stress response, even in the midst of the chaos of daily life. It will help you to reconnect with a feeling of relaxed alertness and emotional equilibrium by getting you out of your head and in touch with your own common sense and deeper wisdom.

Used in conjunction with the hypnotic trance, you will find yourself feeling good in a variety of formerly "stress-full" situations. As you continue to read through the book and do each exercise in turn, you will experience greater joy, relaxation, and well-being in every area of your life.

CHAPTER THREE

•

The Rhythm
of Relaxation

Are You Working Yourself to Death?

> *"Tension is who you think you should be. Relaxation is who you are."*
>
> CHINESE PROVERB

In Japan, stress-related deaths from overworking have become so commonplace that they have their own name—*karoshi*. Unfortunately, this is becoming more and more commonplace here in the West too, as people find themselves overwhelmed by the sheer amount they feel they have to do just to keep up, let alone get ahead.

About ten years ago, I was one of these people. I was working as hard as I could in an effort to get ahead, and I was constantly getting burned out on stress. My body would get ill, and with all the time I wound up having to take off to recover, I realized that pushing myself so hard was a false economy. Even though I got a lot done in my bursts of activity, each time I got ill I'd lose most of the ground I'd gained.

So I decided to take more regular vacations to try to improve my health.

However, I would fill all my time reading books related to my work and going through papers that needed looking at and wouldn't relax in the slightest. I was working just as hard as before, only in a nicer location.

When I began to take a closer look at why I found it so hard to relax, I realized that it was because I was so driven that I didn't want to lose out on any opportunity to get more done. I felt like I was in a race with the rest of the world to succeed. It finally dawned on me that unless I decided to do something completely different, there would never be an end to it. Otherwise, however much I achieved each year, I would just need to achieve more the next.

On one particular vacation, I read a book by Maria Nemeth called *The Energy of Money* that used a phrase I'd never heard before but described my lifestyle far too well for my liking—"Busyholism." This was the idea that sometimes people who feel the need to work all the time because they "need the money" or "can't bear to be bored" are actually addicted to busy-ness. More accurately, they are addicted to the buzz they get from the chemicals their brain produces as a part of the stress response.

For myself, this manifested itself as a feeling of guilt that if I took time off, I would somehow be falling even further behind. Even though I knew rationally that this was not true, I also knew that if I didn't find some way to get around that feeling of guilt, my body would collapse from exhaustion.

I found the answer in an interview I was listening to with sports psychologist Jim Loehr, who worked with many of the top athletes of the day.

In describing the nature of stress in competitive performance in sport, at home, or in the workplace, Loehr explained that if you want to be a peak performer in any area of your life, you have to find ways to renew your energy—physically, emotionally, mentally, and spiritually. Our body's energy systems work best when we turn them on as brightly as we can and then turn them off again.

The metaphor Loehr used was this:

Life is not a marathon—it is a series of sprints.

This is the principle of oscillation—periods of energy expenditure followed by periods of energy recovery. In order to be fully engaged with life at the times when it matters most, we need to be able to switch into recovery mode and give ourselves enough downtime to recharge our system and return to whatever it is we are doing even stronger and more focused than before.

By alternating between periods of intense activity and periods of gentle activity and rest, you can develop your strength and stamina and become more fully engaged with life.

Once I understood the importance of incorporating quality recovery time into my schedule, I began to spend more of my time on vacation just relaxing. I would lie on the beach each day and feel the warmth of the sun on my body, vividly imagining each muscle relaxing from the top of my head all the way down to the tips of my toes.

Even after I returned home, I continued to practice this same technique, but this time I would simply vividly imagine myself sunbathing on an exotic beach. Given that the nervous system does not differentiate between a real and a vividly imagined event, each time I took myself through that experience it felt as though I was still on vacation—and as far as my nervous system was concerned, I was!

The more relaxed I became, the better I felt and the more efficient I became in my work. As I introduced more and more recovery time into my routine, I was able to get more done in less time and I was able to let go of my "addiction" to busy-ness more and more . . .

Natural Cycles of Activity and Rest

One of the simplest ways to build quality recovery time into an already busy schedule is to take advantage of a naturally occurring phenomenon known as the "ultradian rest phase."

Recent research has shown that the mind and body have their own pattern of rest or alertness with one predominant cycle that occurs approximately every 90 minutes. This is when the body stops externally oriented behavior and takes about 15 minutes to relax and replenish its energy.

These are those moments in the day when you find your mind starting to wander and a sweet, soft feeling of relaxation begins to fill your body. It is as though your body is ready to drift off into a wonderful, refreshing sleep.

Unfortunately, many people instantly override this message from their body by choking down a double espresso and trying even harder to concentrate on what they're doing. After a while, they establish a pattern of overriding their body's natural rhythm and the natural feeling of relaxation comes less and less often.

The good news is that all you need to do to bring it back is to allow yourself to take advantage of it when it does occur. For the next week, here is what I want you to do . . .

At least twice a day (if it's safe to do so), when you find yourself daydreaming and a feeling of comfort starting in your body, go with it and allow yourself to relax deeply for no less than five and no more than twenty minutes.

You will awake feeling refreshed and with better concentration afterwards.

You can use the time to listen to the hypnotic trance, or you may like to use the exercise on the next page. It is very simple, but like anything else, the more you practice the better you get.

It simply involves thinking about a particular area of your body and then telling yourself to relax in a soothing tone of voice. Take the time to go through each part of your body slowly, giving yourself time to really feel the tension releasing from that part of your body as you go . . .

SYSTEMATIC RELAXATION

Please read through this exercise first before you do it and remember, do not attempt to do this while driving or operating machinery. Only do it when you can safely relax completely.

1. Use your most comfortable, tired, drowsy voice, as if telling yourself a bedtime story. Simply say each of the following to yourself as you follow your own instructions . . .

   Now I relax my eyes

   Now I relax my jaw

   Now I relax my tongue

   Now I relax my shoulders

   Now I relax my arms

   Now I relax my hands

   Now I relax my chest

   Now I relax my stomach

   Now I relax my thighs

   Now I relax my calves

   Now I relax my feet

   Now I relax my mind

2. Pause for a little while to notice the feelings and then, if you wish, repeat it. Stay with this feeling as long as you wish. You will be able to return to full waking consciousness, refreshed and alert, as soon as you are ready.

The more you practice this technique, the more effective it becomes. You can do it anywhere that you can safely relax and it's discreet. If you do it on the bus or the train, everyone will just think you're dozing. Even if you work in an open-plan office or factory, you can always find an excuse to get out for five minutes.

It may sound like a little thing, hardly worth doing, but taking a couple of five-minute breaks every day as a part of your daily recovery time could be the most valuable thing you ever learn to do.

CHAPTER FOUR

•

The Calm Anchor

Interrupting the Pattern of Stimulus / Response

> *"If you want to know what your thoughts were like yesterday, check how your body feels today."*
>
> INDIAN SAYING

Years ago I did a television program where I was asked by the producers to work with people who had been labeled "incurable."

One was a man with rage disorder. This man was so quick to anger that he had become a danger to himself and others.

Using many of the techniques in this book, I taught him how to get control of his own stress response and how to increase the frequency and depth of his natural relaxation. We practiced relaxing again and again until he could do it in just a few moments by using what we call a "calm anchor."

In the same way as the anchor of a boat helps keep it steady in the midst of stormy seas, an emotional anchor helps you to stay calm in the midst of your daily life. But unlike the anchor of a boat, an emotional anchor actually gets stronger the more you use it.

Do you remember the story of Pavlov's dogs?

The Russian scientist Ivan Pavlov conditioned his dogs to salivate each time he rang a bell. Every time he fed them, he would ring a bell. Once that association between the bell and the food was "anchored" into their nervous systems, he could simply ring the bell and they would begin to respond as if they were about to be fed.

The two exercises you are about to do make use of this same kind of associative conditioning and will help you to cultivate an inner calm as a regular part of your daily life. You can also use them to spread the feeling of relaxed alertness into more and more areas of your life . . .

THE CALM ANCHOR

Before you do this technique for yourself, read through each step so that you know exactly what to do.

1. Remember a time when you felt really, really calm—at peace and in control. Fully return to it now, seeing what you saw, hearing what you heard and feeling how good you felt. (If you can't remember a time, imagine how wonderful it would feel to be totally at peace—if you had all the ease, comfort, and self-control you could ever need!)

2. As you keep running through this experience in your mind, make the colors brighter and richer, the sounds crisper, and the feelings stronger. When you are feeling these good feelings, squeeze the thumb and middle finger of your **right hand** together. You are associating this particular pressure in this particular place with this particular emotion. Run through this memory several times until you feel a lovely sense of inner peace and calm.

3. Now go through this relaxing memory at least five more times while continuing to squeeze your thumb and middle finger together to really lock in these good feelings. You will know you have done it enough when all you need to do is squeeze your fingers together and you can easily remember the feelings of calm and relaxation spreading through your body.

4. Next, think about a situation that in the past you would have found mildly stressful. (We will

deal with any "high-stress" situations in the next exercise.) Once again, squeeze your thumb and middle finger together. Feel that calm feeling spreading through your body and imagine taking it with you into that stressful situation. Imagine everything going perfectly, exactly the way that you want. See what you'll see, hear what you hear, and feel how good it feels to be so much calmer and in control in this situation.

5. Now, still squeezing your thumb and finger together, remember that calm feeling of being in control and once again imagine being in that situation that used to seem stressful. This time, imagine a few challenges occurring and notice yourself handling all the challenges perfectly. See what you'll see, hear what you hear, and feel how good it feels to be so much calmer and in control in this situation.

6. Stop and think about that situation now. Notice the difference from only a few minutes ago. Do you feel less stressed and more in control? If not, just repeat the exercise until you do!

Each time you do this exercise, it will become easier and easier to experience feelings of relaxation and calm "at your fingertips" . . .

When you feel comfortable with this exercise, you are ready to reprogram yourself to be generally more relaxed—to trigger your natural relaxation response at will and experience a greater sense of ease and well-being in any area of your life.

Remember, your nervous system cannot tell the difference between a real and vividly imagined experience. So each time in the past that you imagined a stressful situation, you experienced that stress almost as much as if it were really happening now.

By imagining those same situations but this time responding with inner calm instead of stress, you are reprogramming yourself to feel calmer and more in control in every area of your life. As you begin to feel better and better, you will be able to handle all those situations more effectively in the future.

CONTROL YOUR STRESS FOR LIFE

Before you do this technique for yourself, read through each step so that you know exactly what to do.

1. What I want you to do is to pick the five most significant stresses currently active in your life. Actually write them down to make it easier to re- member them as you go through the following. Once you've created your list, we are going to sys- tematically lower the stress levels on each one of them. This will create a new generalization in your unconscious mind, leading to a lower overall stress level in your life.

2. Choose one of the five situations to begin the pro- cess of change. Now, using the calm anchor you created in the previous exercise, think about this sit- uation you normally find stressful and squeeze your thumb and finger together. Feel that calm feeling spreading through your body and imagine taking it with you into that stressful situation. Imagine everything going perfectly, exactly the way that you want. See what you'll see, hear what you hear, and feel how good it feels to be so much calmer and in control in this situation.

3. Now, still squeezing your thumb and finger to- gether, remember that calm feeling of being in control and once again imagine being in that situation that used to seem stressful. This time, imagine a few challenges occurring and notice yourself handling all the challenges perfectly. See what you'll see, hear what you hear, and feel how good it feels to be so much calmer and in control in this situation.

4. Stop and think about that situation now. Notice the difference from only a few minutes ago. Do you feel less stressed and more in control? If not, just repeat the exercise until you do!

5. Repeat this process with each one of the five situations until you feel significantly more relaxed and in control. The process of generalization has now begun!

The more you do this exercise, the easier it will get. And the more you listen to the *Instant Calm* audio download, the more deeply you will be able to relax and the more good feelings you will begin to feel.

CHAPTER FIVE

•

The Ultimate
Stress Reliever

Exercise Is Good for You—Who Knew?

> *"Lack of activity destroys the good condition of every human being, while movement and methodical physical exercise save it and preserve it."*
>
> PLATO

I got a call recently from an old friend who had been caught up in the credit crunch and was, in his own words, "stressed to the max." After he had told me how difficult he was finding it to cope, I asked him how much exercise he was getting.

He seemed surprised by the question, but he told me that he hadn't gotten any exercise since things had gone wrong with the stock market, as he needed all his available time to "make things happen."

I asked him to just try one thing before we spoke again—do at least 20 minutes of physical exercise twice a day over the next three days. By the time we next spoke, he had his stress back under control and had made a breakthrough in his thinking about his business.

We live in an age when incredible medical advancements are constantly taking place. Drugs and surgery have become commonplace. Many people expect instant cures from the doctors for their ills and hand over responsibility for their health to the medical profession, preferring a prescription to instigating a change in their lifestyle or diet.

However, one of the single most powerful tools we all have in our grasp to control stress is to exercise. By exercise, I mean any activity that gets your heart pumping faster than usual and your lungs breathing more deeply.

For years now, exercise has been prescribed in clinical settings to help treat nervous tension. Research has shown that not only do patients exhibit a decrease in the electrical activity of tensed muscles, they appear less jittery and hyperactive afterwards.

What this kind of exercise does is improve blood flow to the brain and major organs of the body, in the process speeding up the elimination of adrenaline, cortisol, and other chemicals that have been released into the bloodstream as part of the stress response. It also triggers natural relaxation, flooding the body with endorphins that can lead to a sort of post-exercise euphoria sometimes referred to as "runner's high."

Swimming, running, lifting weights, doing yoga, or even going for a bike ride will all make it easier to control your stress and experience more positive feelings. However, in most cases you can create the same benefits of more strenuous exercise by simply going for a 15-minute walk once or twice a day.

One of the early success stories from the *I Can Make You Thin* system has been Yvonne Meaney, who lost almost 80 pounds and at the time of writing has kept it off for over four years. When she began, she never exercised, so she started out by simply taking the dog for a short walk each morning. One thing led to another, and she has now run four complete marathons!

The reason something like this can happen is that exercise is a self-reinforcing activity. Because of all the positive physical effects, the more you do the more your body begins to crave it. As your stamina increases, it gets easier and easier to do until you reach a tipping point—a point in time where it actually becomes easier to do it than not. The easier it gets and the more you want to do it, the more of it you do and the benefits keep increasing.

Far too many people start an exercise program and then give up within a week because they've set the bar too high—they've literally tried to run before they can walk. As long as you do *something* each and every day, even if it's only a quick stroll around the block when you get home from the office or taking the stairs when you would normally have taken the elevator, you will be surprised at how quickly you begin to feel better.

Just Do It!

Exercise helps you to build muscle, lose fat, and feel great. It contributes to clearer skin, enhanced mental clarity, better athletic performance, and an increased sex drive. Certain hormones released during exercise have been shown to slow and even reverse the aging process.

So if you aren't already exercising regularly, it's probably because your perception of exercise involves seeing yourself huffing and puffing on an exercise machine, listening to a maniacal aerobics drill instructor shouting "feel the burn," or looking into a wall-sized mirror surrounded by people who look so much better than you that you just want to go home and throw up.

But when we're talking about controlling stress, the goal isn't to get fit—it's to get fit for life. It doesn't matter what you look like before, during, or after—it's about how it makes you feel. And the more you enjoy it, the more you'll do it.

In the next exercise, we are going to reshape your perception of exercise to make it much more appealing, using the same anchoring process you learned in the last chapter.

You can also listen to the hypnotic trance that comes with this book as often as you like. The more you listen, the more motivated to exercise you will become.

Just by taking the time to complete this exercise, you will set in motion the awesome power of momentum in your life. Whatever you set your mind on doing will be easier to achieve than ever before, because you are now going to put yourself in charge of your own motivation . . .

INSTANT MOTIVATION

In a moment we are going to remember some times when you felt totally motivated, or anything else that you REALLY enjoyed doing. Then we are going to create an association between those feelings and making a fist with your dominant hand, over and over again.

1. Rate on a scale of 1–10 how strong your motivation to exercise is. 1 is the weakest, 10 the strongest.

2. Think of something you are already motivated to do. It may be something you feel particularly passionate about, like your favorite hobby or pastime, a political cause, being with a loved one, or spending time with your family. If nothing springs to mind immediately ask yourself, if you had won a lottery jackpot—how motivated would you be to go and claim the check? Or how motivated would you be to save the life of your closest friend? Or if the most attractive person in the world asked you out on a date—how motivated would you be to say yes?

3. Whatever motivates you most right now, I'd like you to visualize the scene—seeing it through your own eyes as though it's here now. See again what you see, hear what you hear, and feel exactly how being motivated feels.

    > Now notice all the details of the scene, make the colors richer, bolder, and brighter. Make the sounds clearer and the feelings stronger. As the feelings build to a peak, make a fist with your dominant hand.

4. Keep going through that motivational movie. As soon as it finishes, start it again, all the time feeling that motivation and squeezing your hand together into a fist. See what you saw, hear what you heard, and feel that motivation.

5. STOP! Relax your hand and move around a bit.

   Now, are you ready to test your motivation trigger? Squeeze your fist and relive that good feeling now. It's important to realize it may not feel as intense, but you can increase your feelings of motivation every time you do this exercise.

6. It's time to make the association between feeling motivated and moving your body. Make a fist and remember what it's like to feel motivated. Now imagine yourself moving your body easily and effortlessly throughout the day. Imagine things going perfectly, going exactly the way you want them to go, finding more and more opportunities to enjoy moving your body in enjoyable ways. See what you'll see, hear what you'll hear, and feel how good it feels. As soon as you have done that go through it again, still making that fist, permanently associating motivation with exercise.

7. Finally, on a scale of 1–10, how motivated do you feel to exercise? The higher the number, the easier you will find it to incorporate into your daily routine. The lower the number, the more you need to practice the preceding technique.

CHAPTER SIX

•

Positively Worrying

All about Worry

> "How much pain
> they have cost us,
> the evils which have
> never happened."
>
> THOMAS JEFFERSON

What's your biggest worry right now?

- Is it something to do with your finances or job?

- Are you worried about your physical health or the health of someone close to you?

- Do you obsess over something that happened in the past or that you fear may happen in the future?

The word "worry" comes from a Greek word that can be translated as "divided mind." And that is exactly what worry feels like so much of the time—a stream of thoughts pulling you in many different directions at once.

Worrying is not only one of the least productive uses we can make of our minds, it is one of the least pleasant. So why do we keep on worrying?

When I ask this question of people in my seminars, they invariably answer in one of two ways:

1. They believe that in some way worrying keeps them safe.

2. They believe that they don't know how to stop.

Fortunately, both of these beliefs are based on inaccurate and incomplete information.

Does worrying *always* keep you safe? Have you never been able to let go of a worrying thought?

We are designed as human beings to keep things familiar and stay in control as best we can. But there is a tremendous difference between taking care of what is within your control and worrying about what is not.

A few years ago, I had the opportunity to interview a number of the wealthiest people on the planet for my book *I Can Make You Rich*, including Sir Richard Branson, Sir Philip Green, and Dame Anita Roddick. One of the things that struck me about them was their sense of calm, even in the face of decisions that could make or cost their companies millions of dollars.

When I asked them about it, they each shared with me their own version of a process they used that is known as "downside planning," which essentially works like this:

1. Think about an upcoming event or transaction.

2. Imagine all the things that could possibly go wrong with that thing.

3. Come up with a solution for each eventuality.

What is fascinating is this:

What most people call "worrying" is simply interrupting the process of downside planning after the second step!

That is, people imagine all the things that could possibly go wrong *but never get around to creating solutions*.

I experienced this firsthand recently when a very successful actor who has worked in numerous films and television productions approached me one day to hypnotize him not to worry anymore.

When I asked him for more information, he told me that he was rehearsing a play and was becoming increasingly worried about his seeming inability to learn his lines. That worry in turn was making it harder and harder to learn the lines, and as opening night was fast approaching the worry was quickly turning into panic.

But when I offered to help him learn his lines more quickly, he just seemed confused.

"I don't want help learning my lines—I want you to make me stop worrying."

I pointed out that, as with downside planning, the trick to stopping worry in its tracks is to solve whatever problem it is you are worrying about to the best of your ability. If that makes the worry go away, then you know it was just a message from your emotional intelligence to better prepare you for the task at hand.

If the worry continues even after you've come up with a viable solution for the problem, then chances are it's just an overactive protection mechanism with a faulty reset button. Listening to the hypnotic trance on a regular basis and/or using the Worry Buster technique in the next chapter will reset the mechanism and allow you to sort out what's worth worrying about. What you'll quickly find out is that not much is.

Of course, not all problems even need to be solved. A fascinating study first reported by author and researcher

Jay Haley into waiting lists for therapy showed that over 50 percent of people got better *before* they finally got in to see the therapist. This points to the fact that much of what people worry about would take care of itself if people simply gave it the time and space to resolve.

A friend of mine who was moved to LA from London by his company echoed this when he told me that he'd once heard that most business problems are solved or resolved by 3 p.m. of the day they are discovered. Since the time difference meant that his business day now did not begin until 3 p.m. London time, he found that many of the problems that he had been e-mailed about in the night had been solved by the time he showed up for work!

How to Solve Even the Most Difficult of Problems

When I was a child being taught in school, they told us that the world's oil would run out by the year 2000. However, what hadn't been taken into consideration was the ingenuity of the human mind.

Within a few years, the development of fuel-injection systems and alternative drilling and refinement processes meant that not only was there more oil available, we were able to get more than twice as much out of every barrel. Now, new creative innovations have led to the development of more renewable and sustainable energy sources.

The human mind is like a problem-solving machine, and its seemingly infinite creative ability has led to continual innovation and development in the fields of art, science, architecture, medicine, and more. In fact, some people say that the only limit to the creativity of the human mind lies in people's beliefs about what's possible.

One of my favorite examples of the ability of the mind to solve problems when unfettered by a limiting belief is the story of George Bernard Dantzig, a student who arrived late for a math class and saw two problems written on the blackboard. Assuming they were the day's homework, he jotted them down, but found it took him longer than expected to actually solve them.

When he handed in his homework a few days late, his teacher seemed taken aback, and Dantzig quickly apologized, explaining that "they were a bit more difficult than usual."

The equations he had solved had not been meant as homework at all—they were two famously "unsolvable" problems of statistics. Because Dantzig didn't know he wasn't supposed to be able to solve them, he was able to bring the full power of his creative mind to the problem. His work was later published in academic papers and his story became legend.

The point is this:

When you tap into the genius and creativity of your mind, solving even the most difficult problems becomes possible.

Here are the two steps to all effective problem-solving tools:

1. Put yourself into a calmer, more relaxed state of mind and put everything that's going on into a new, more positive perspective.

2. Begin generating solutions!

There is a scientific principle called "the law of requisite variety," which says that "the part of a system that has the most flexibility ends up in control of the system."

In other words, in any given environment, from a corporation to a family to a political party, the person who has the most flexibility in their thinking and behaviors will be the most influential person.

Or to put it even more simply:

> **The more ways of looking at something you have, the more choices you have.**
> **The more choices you have, the more likely you will end up in control.**

Each of the creative problem solvers that follow offer you new ways of looking at problems, giving you new choices and ultimately greater control. They will help you to eliminate the vast majority of your worries by taking your attention off the "problem" and placing it on the solution or solutions.

Be sure to take at least one of your worries through each of these techniques so you become familiar with how it works. Then you will be able to make use of them any time in the future where you find yourself stuck in a seemingly endless loop of worry.

PROBLEM-SOLVING TECHNIQUE 1

The Problem-Solving Questions

Over the years, I've learned that a good question is worth its weight in gold, not only for the answers it draws forth but also for the positive frame of mind it can help you to get into.

Several years ago, I was introduced to six simple questions from the field of decision theory that can help you to solve any problem.

In order to put these questions to work for you, simply choose a problem, concern, or worry and answer each question as honestly as you can.

1.   What are three positive things about this problem?

2.   What's not yet the way you want it?

3.   What are you willing to do to get the result you want?

4.   What are you willing to stop doing to get the result you want?

5. How can you motivate yourself and even take pleasure in doing what needs to be done to get the result you want?

6. What's something you can do today to get things moving in the right direction?

Each time you ask and answer these questions, you will gain new insights into how to better handle the situation you are exploring.

PROBLEM-SOLVING TECHNIQUE 2

Role Model Step-In

Sometimes the difference that makes the difference in solving problems is not looking at the situation in a different way, but rather looking at it with different eyes.

We have all had the experience of getting stuck with a problem and asking someone else for their opinion. They then point something out that up until that moment we had not seen, but once we see it becomes obvious to us.

Here's all you need to do to give yourself a whole new insight into your problems and begin generating positive solutions:

1. Think of somebody who is good at solving problems and sorting things out. The person you choose can be real or a character from a story. Over the years, I have seen people choose everyone from Sherlock Holmes to Arnold Schwarzenegger and from Albert Einstein to their Auntie Doris. All that matters is that you have a strong enough sense of what they are like that you can imagine them vividly in your mind.

2. Now, take a few moments to imagine yourself seeing the world through your problem-solver's eyes. See what they would see and hear what they would hear.

3. While still looking through their eyes, think about a particular problem you have and consider it from this point of view. How would they handle it if it was their problem? What advice would they give to you about it? What do they think is the best course of action?

4. Act on any insights you may have!

PROBLEM-SOLVING TECHNIQUE 3

Back to the Future

One of the most unusual sessions I ever did was with a woman who seemed completely unresponsive to every technique I used with her. I had no idea what to do, so I asked her to imagine going out into a time in the future when her problem had already been solved. I then asked her future self to tell me what I had done to solve it. To my surprise, she was able to answer my question in great detail.

When she reoriented herself in the present, I applied the strategy she had explained to me. Less than an hour later, her problem was gone!

Here's a simple way for you to use this same process for yourself:

1. Imagine yourself some time in the future when this problem has already been solved.

2. Look back towards the present and ask yourself, "What happened? How did this problem get solved? What did I do to contribute to the solution?"

3. Allow yourself to act on any insights you may have.

Remember, it is not important that you get a clear answer. Simply by viewing the problem from the perspective of the future, it will begin to change!

CHAPTER SEVEN

•

Making Peace
with Your Mind

What's the Use of Worrying?

> *"We can never obtain peace in the outer world until we make peace with ourselves."*
>
> THE DALAI LAMA

Although we have already seen how most worry is simply a halfway house on the way to a creative solution, sometimes knowing what can be done still isn't enough to stop the train of worry thoughts in its tracks.

For example, I worked with a lady recently who was constantly worried about her young children getting out onto the street and being hit by a car. She was being tortured by her own mind, living through 30 road accidents a day in her head and constantly obsessing over whether the front gate was locked.

Although her "worry habit" was consuming her life and had begun to affect her health, when I asked her if it would be okay with her if we took her worry away, she looked terrified.

Because I know that all behavior has a positive intention, I asked her in what way she believed that her worry was serving her. She told me, "I worry to keep my children safe."

Now, we all can recognize that there's a huge difference between being a good and caring mother and stressing yourself out to the point of exhaustion. After making sure that she was already taking every reasonable precaution to keep her children safe, I pointed out to her that although the intention of her mind was positive, it was overdoing its job.

One simple way to get a better understanding of the function of worry is to look at where it sits on the following scale:

```
←——0------1------2------3------4------5——→
    Apathy   Interest   Concern   Worry   Panic
```

At one end of the scale is apathy and indifference; at the other are panic attacks and generalized anxiety disorder.

```
←——0------1------2------3------4------5——→
    Apathy   Interest   Concern   Worry   Panic
```

In an ideal world, we want to stay towards the middle of the scale, between 2 and 3, maintaining enough healthy interest and concern to make sure that everything that needs to get done gets done, but not allowing ourselves to get caught up in worry or panic about those things that are outside of our control.

However, this particular woman's thermostat of concern was set so high that she lived in a constant state of fear.

Resolving Internal Conflict

Have you ever had the experience of wanting two seemingly conflicting things to happen simultaneously?

Perhaps one part of you wanted to go out to a bar while another part wanted to stay in and prepare for the next day's "big event," or part of you wanted to be thin while another part wanted to polish off a dozen donuts and 16 pints of beer. In most cases, whichever part has the strongest intention will determine which choices get made.

Now it's not as though there are actually little "parts" running around inside of us, determining what we do and don't do all day long. The idea of "parts" is just a simple way of understanding the different aspects of our personality.

In the case of the worried mother, a part of her thought that continual and excessive worrying was the best way to keep her children safe. This "worrying" part wanted the best for her and her kids, but was going about getting it in an unproductive and ultimately self-destructive way.

So I asked the part of her responsible for the worry to find ways of making sure her children were safe without having to continually evoke the stress response in her.

After a few moments, she was able to imagine a number of simple ways she could care for her children's well-being without all the hypervigilance and obsessive behavior she had been demonstrating up until that point.

Even before we completed the exercise, I could see her body relax as she was able to let go of the worry while continuing to do her best for her children.

Here is a version of the exercise I did with that woman that you can use for yourself to eliminate worry without losing out on any of the positive benefits that the worry was designed to create . . .

THE WORRY BUSTER

Read the instructions all the way through once—then go back and go through each step in order . . .

1. Think about something you have been worrying about.

2. Ask yourself: "What is the positive intention of this worry? What is it doing for me? What does it do for me, get me, or give me?" Very often, the answer will simply be some variation on "to keep me safe."

3. When you've got an answer that feels right to you, ask your mind to come up with at least three new ways that you could get all the positive benefit of the worry without having to take on the stress and uncomfortable feelings.

4. Check to make sure that you are completely comfortable with taking on these new alternatives to worrying. If there is any hesitation, go back to your mind and ask it to sort out any internal conflicts. You will know you're ready to move on when you are feeling completely at peace with your new alternatives.

Imagine what it will be like doing those new things instead of worrying in the future until it seems almost familiar to you, as if that's what you've always done!

Going through this exercise will reset your worry thermostat and allow you to make the shift from panic and worry to interest and concern.

After you have run through it a few times, you will find that the pattern begins to generalize. You will notice that you are worrying less and less but still taking care of everything that needs to get done.

In the hypnotic trance, I will guide your unconscious mind through this exercise in a number of different ways. Each time you listen, the new pattern will get stronger and it will be easier and easier for you to let go of any unnecessary worry.

By continuing to use the hypnotic trance every single day, we will also be reprogramming your mind to make better use of the amazing biocomputer between your ears, teaching it how to make better decisions and solve nearly any problem in a matter of minutes.

CHAPTER EIGHT

•

What's Your Story?

Stories Are Everywhere

> *"Adopting the right attitude can convert a negative stress into a positive one."*
>
> HANS SELYE

Throughout history, stories have been the fabric of our society. From Greek mythology and the teaching stories of Jesus and the Buddha to Aesop's fables and the plays of Shakespeare, stories are there to guide and instruct us on every facet of our lives. Today, some of our best storytellers—people like Steven Spielberg, J. K. Rowling, and Dan Brown—are among the highest-paid people of our time.

Even something as seemingly factual as the news is just a story of what happened in the world today, and the news outlets tell you a story about the facts that give you ways of making sense of world events. But whether you agree with their particular way of telling the story or not, it's still just a story.

At the bar, listening to your friends, it's the story of their lives, the story of work, the story of their past, the story of the world. Some stories are positive and some are negative—they can lift us up or bring us down.

But the most important story of all is the one you tell yourself about yourself and your life—the story of you.

All day long we talk to ourselves, making sense of our life and the world around us. Everyone is telling themselves a story all day long about what life, and their life in particular, is all about. These stories have been shaped by our upbringing and the stories we witnessed and were told growing up, especially the first six or seven years of life.

If as you were growing up you were repeatedly told that life is a struggle, chances are that is your experience. If you were taught that it was a game, that's how you probably play it. People tend to look at the world through the filter of their stories, and consequently that's all they see around them.

So if you've ever wondered why "things like this" always happen to you, one of the best places to look is at how whatever's happening fits into the story of your life.

The Story of Stress and Worry

Remember the old TV commercials that went, "We won't create a drama out of a crisis"?

What that means is that even when bad things happen, you don't have to make them worse by adding in a bleak and tragic story.

Yet many people have been telling themselves their own story so compellingly that they are literally hypnotized by it—it's become so real to them that they're unable to even see it as a story anymore.

What are the things you tell yourself that stress you out?

- *I never have enough time.*

- *I can't cope.*

- *The world would stop if I have a day off.*

- *I have a stressful job.*

- *I'm a perfectionist—I need things to be a certain way.*

- *Nobody else could handle all the things I have to put up with.*

Remember, not all stories are negative. If you've spent your life telling yourself that you're a gifted learner, a loyal friend and a "get it done" kind of person, chances are that story has served you well.

But in our culture, the more common stories are imposed upon us from the outside. If you've ever been told that you're "just no good at math," or that you're "shy," or "you'll never amount to anything," chances are you've struggled in those areas. At some point, you probably took on the story as your own and began repeating it in your head and out loud to others, using the label as a part of your identity and building further stories around it to support it.

And while there may be some truth in these stories, the more we tell them to ourselves and others, the more we believe them and the more real they begin to seem.

But they are all still just stories. And the most wonderful thing about a story is that it can be changed, often more easily than you think.

And the only thing you need to do to change your story is to recognize that it *is* a story.

I told the story in *I Can Make You Sleep* of the client I was working with who said to me, "I just can't sleep, I'm an insomniac."

"That's what you tell yourself," I replied.

"No," he said, "you don't understand, I really am an insomniac."

"That's what you tell yourself," I said again.

We repeated this little exchange three or four times before he realized he was actually hearing what he was telling himself.

"Right," he said, "that is what I'm telling myself."

"So now," I asked him, "would you like to tell yourself something different?"

As long as you believe your story is real, you'll look outside yourself to make changes. Once you can see that your story, no matter how compelling it may seem, is just the sum total of what you've been telling yourself, you open up the possibility of making changes on the inside that will literally change your world.

If your story says that you are defined by what you have done in the past, you will almost certainly repeat that past on into the future. If you tell yourself a new story about how it's possible to begin doing things differently in any moment, you can change your future, starting right now.

The point is this:

What you've thought of as your limitations are just a story you tell yourself. You can change that story in any moment.

LETTING GO OF THE STORY OF STRESS AND WORRY

I'm now going to show you how to let go, stage by stage, of any old worry stories you may be telling yourself so that your natural emotional equilibrium can return to balance.

1. Think about a situation you have been stressing and/or worrying about.
2. Now, begin to notice what you've been telling yourself about that situation.

    *   "There's nothing I can do, it's happening again."

    *   "I can't change, it runs in the family."

    *   "I'm just not up to this."

    *   "Why does this kind of thing always happen to me?"

    If you're not aware of anything that you're telling yourself, it's okay to make it up!

3. Now, really hear that inner voice and notice where it is coming from. The front, side, or back of your head?
4. Imagine floating those words out of your head and imagine hearing those words as though they are the voice-over of a movie coming from somewhere about 12 feet away from you. Hear it as if they are coming from over there now.

5. As you hear the voice telling you that old story from 12 feet away, notice how different it feels to hear it like that.

6. This simple difference allows your mind to recalibrate its interpretation and frees you from identifying with that story. Hearing that voice over there means there is now room for a different story over here.

7. Now, as gradually as you like, turn down the volume of that story over there.

8. Notice that you are now free to tell yourself a new story—a story of possibility, hope, and power. You may want to write down your new story or even speak it out loud. The more you repeat your new story, the more real it will start to become for you.

CHAPTER NINE

•

Changing the Way You See the World

The Picture of Stress

> *"If you are distressed by anything external, the pain is not due to the thing itself, but to your estimate of it; and this you have the power to revoke at any moment."*
>
> MARCUS AURELIUS

One of the key determining factors in how we feel from moment to moment is the pictures we're making in our imagination and the stories we are telling ourselves in our mind. These internal images and sounds are going on all day long, like a television program left on in the background as you walk around your home or office.

However, even if you have never consciously practiced seeing or working with the pictures in your head, it is an ability that is already within you.

- Imagine you are standing outside the front door of your home. What color is the door? Is the handle on the right or on the left?

- Picture a lemon in front of you. Now imagine slicing into it, and then biting into the juicy insides.

Did you know what side of your door the handle was on? Did your mouth begin to pucker at the thought of biting into that lemon?

Then you are sufficiently in touch with your internal imagery to benefit from the rest of the techniques in this book, and you will find it easier and easier as you practice more and more. Simply do each one of the imagination exercises that follow to the best of your ability and listen to the hypnotic trance repeatedly—in just one week's time you will be amazed by how different your experience has already become!

The Difference That Makes All the Difference in the World

I remember when I first started working with clients, a man came to me who was clearly on the edge with stress and worry. When I asked him what it was about, he said there were three things he was dealing with and that he was running each one over and over in his mind.

As he told me about each one in turn, I noticed that as he described them he gestured as if the things he was describing were all around him there in the room with us. It was clear that he wasn't just thinking about these things—his memories were so real to him that he was living inside each one as if it was happening to him now.

So I asked him to stop for a moment and to float up out of each scenario and look at it from a distance, seeing himself in the pictures almost as if those things were happening to someone else. Gradually, I could see the muscles around his eyes and jaw begin to relax and the color return to his cheeks. Soon, he looked considerably more relaxed.

I then asked him to think about each one of his problems from this new, relaxed place and to ask himself what (if anything) he needed to do about each one. He told me afterwards he was flooded with insights, but the most important one was the realization that everything was okay and there was absolutely nothing for him to worry about.

Over the years, I've found that one of the most powerful shifts you can make in your perceptions is to step inside or outside your internal imagery. The process of stepping outside of a thought or memory is called "dissociation," and mastering it will not only instantly reduce your stress, it will give you a greater experience of control and freedom in your life.

Here is all you need to do . . .

DISSOCIATION

1. Think of a *mildly* stressful or uncomfortable situation or memory.

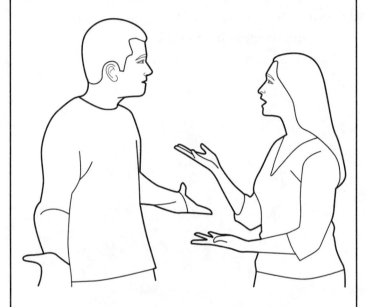

2. As you notice what image or images come to mind, float out of yourself so you can see the back of your head. Pull back from that image and float it as far away from you as you can so you can see yourself way over there, still in it.

3. Drain all color out of the image and make it black and white, faint and transparent.

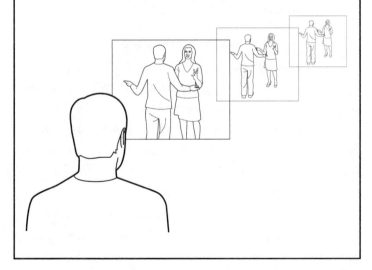

The process of dissociating reduces the intensity of the feelings the images in your mind were creating. This is one of the basic operating principles of the mind:

- To increase the emotional intensity of a memory or imagined event, "associate" into an image so that you are seeing what you would see, hearing what you would hear, and feeling the way you would feel if you were actually there.

- To decrease the emotional intensity of a memory or imagined event, "dissociate" from the imagery so that you can see it from the outside, as if it's happening to someone else "over there."

As we learn to associate into more and more of our positive memories and dissociate from the negative, we increase our well-being, reduce our stress and get a completely different perspective on our lives.

And since the main trigger for the stress response is NOT what happens but rather our perception of what happens, we can learn to control our perceptions and in so doing to control our stress.

Here is an exercise you can do that will give you greater mastery over your perceptions and allow you to reduce your stress in any moment . . .

TAKING CONTROL OF YOUR OWN MIND

Before you do this technique for yourself, read through each step so that you know exactly what to do.

1. Think about something you have been finding stressful. Bring it to mind and picture it now. It may be something from the past that still bothers you, or something you have been worrying about in the future. You may see it as a few pictures—for example, someone's face or a room full of people—or you may see it as a sort of mini-video—a film of something happening or people watching you and talking. It doesn't matter what sort of picture or video it is—just see it in your mind however it looks to you.

2. Next, step out of the image like a special effect in a movie—in other words, imagine floating out of yourself, so that you can see the back of your head as you float further and further away until you can see yourself in the picture.

3. Now, float the image away from you another 12 feet so you can see that stressful situation like it's happening to someone else.

4. Next, drain out all the color from the image until it's only in black and white, like a very old movie.

5. Now shrink it down in size until it's a lot smaller.

6. Keep watching it and make it as transparent as you can.

7. Finally, now that the emotional intensity has been reduced, ask yourself if you need to make any decisions about the situation. If you do, make those decisions from this new perspective.

CHAPTER TEN

•

Healing the Past

Out at the edge of the stress response

> "It's never too late to have a happy childhood."
>
> TOM ROBBINS

"Post-traumatic stress disorder" is a term coined in the 1970s to describe the condition formerly known as "shell shock." Symptoms include flashbacks and nightmares, difficulty falling or staying asleep, anger, and hypervigilance.

In my work with people who have suffered serious trauma, I am consistently amazed at the wide range of responses people have to what happens to them. With soldiers in particular, I have noticed that two people can go through the same horrific ordeal and yet come away with completely different experiences.

The difference comes in the way they interpreted the events—that is, in the particular combination of images, sounds, words and feelings their brains have used to represent the memory. This is why some people are left in a world of waking nightmares by a traumatic incident and others bounce back seemingly more resilient than ever before.

While we might think that stress would be the natural consequence of having gone through an extremely traumatic event, I have had the opportunity to see up close how a shift in the perception of an event really can make the difference between heaven and hell in terms of our response to that event.

I was at a dinner party a few years ago when I noticed that the lady sitting opposite me looked stressed and unwell. When I asked her what was wrong, she explained that she had recently been in a motorcycle accident in Thailand. She said that she couldn't stop thinking about it and hadn't slept properly in over two weeks.

While this was clearly a horrific incident, I could see that she was now physically okay. This let me know that the only reason she was still so disturbed was that her internal re-presentation of the accident was not a useful one.

When I asked her what specifically she had been thinking about that was upsetting her, she told me that she kept seeing the bike on top of her and blood on the road. As she spoke, she gestured so that I could see exactly where she was making the pictures, and from the way she talked about it and the emotional reaction she was having, it was clear that she was associated into the picture and running it like a movie in her mind, over and over again.

Even though the accident had only happened once in the real world, she had relived it in her imagination again and again.

I asked her to stop and float out of the picture, so she could see the back of her head as she sent the still image of that unhappy memory far away across to the other side of the room. She began to see it almost as though it had happened to someone else. Then I asked her to shrink the image down to the size of a postage stamp, then to drain all the color out so it became like an old black-and-white photograph. For the first time since I had met her, she looked relaxed.

Then I used a special technique developed by Dr. Richard Bandler to permanently disconnect the feelings of upset and trauma from the memory of what happened. When she was dissociated from the traumatic movie, I asked her to play it backwards as fast as she could, from the point just after the trauma was over and she knew she had survived it, all the way back to the moment before it had occurred.

We did this several times, faster and faster until it recoded the experience in her mind. She could still remember what happened, but she could no longer get upset about it in the same way. Although she still knew that something bad had happened, she was no longer a victim of it.

The whole thing took ten minutes, not ten months of therapy and not even ten seconds of re-experiencing the pain of the traumatic event. She called me a couple of weeks later and said that she had been sleeping fine and was no longer haunted by the memory.

While not everyone can change every traumatic memory that quickly, it is surprising how often they can. I never cease to be amazed at how quickly a human being can change when the right approach is used.

While dealing with a trauma requires professional assistance, you can use this same technique to free yourself from any recurring or persistent memories or worries . . .

REWIRING AN UNPLEASANT MEMORY

Read the instructions all the way through one time—then go back and go through each step in order . . .

Disclaimer: If you even suspect that you are suffering from the aftereffects of a trauma, you must seek professional advice. Do not use the following technique! If in any doubt, consult your doctor or medical professional first.

1. Imagine that you are in a comfortable movie theater. Sit down in the most comfortable chair you can find—the kind that you would almost be concerned you might fall asleep in if the movie was a bit boring.

2. Now, imagine that you can float up out of your body and into the projection booth. Stand behind the solid glass of the projection booth and look down into the theater until you can see the back of your head down there, looking up at the movie screen.

3. You are going to watch a film of the traumatic memory. However, before you do, mark two spots in the film—a few frames before the event ever happened, and another a few frames after you successfully came out on the other side of whatever that event was.

4. Place a still image of the BEFORE frame up onto the screen. Safely behind the solid glass of the projection booth, watch yourself down in the comfy theater watching the film of what happened up on the screen all the way to the moment AFTER you successfully came out on the other side of whatever that event was. When you get to the end, freeze the AFTER image up on the screen.

5. Now, run the film backwards as fast as you can. See all the images going backwards, the sound running backwards, everything moving in reverse, all the way back to the beginning before it ever happened.

6. Repeat steps 4 and 5 at least three times until the memory has lost its emotional impact.

You will know that the technique has worked when you can think about the situation without bringing back the uncomfortable feelings. Listening regularly to the hypnotic trance will also help you to clean up any additional memories or worries you may still be experiencing in less than useful ways.

CHAPTER ELEVEN

•

The Art of Being

All Toys, No Joy

> "If you want to be happy, be."
>
> LEO TOLSTOY

I never cease to be amazed at the number of people I have met or worked with as clients who have so much—wealth, busy fast-moving lives—and yet are so stressed and miserable. They have all the toys but none of the joy of a wealthy life.

On the other hand, I meet people nearly every day who have far less but are able to enjoy their lives far more. This is not to say that having nice things makes you unhappy. It's just that unless you deliberately cultivate your inner resources, you will never find the peace of mind that we all crave in one way or another.

Making all the changes you want in the outside world—finding a new partner or a better job, making more money and driving a bigger car—means very little if you haven't first learned to relax and live peacefully on the inside. It's a bit like rearranging the deck chairs on the *Titanic*—it might make things look better to others, but inside, the whole ship is still going down!

One of my own wake-up calls in this area came in the form of a visit from a friend who is a Zen master. As we spent time together, I became more and more impressed at how relaxed he seemed. He radiated a sense of calm and well-being that seemed a stark contrast to my busy, high-achiever pace.

Yet he had just as much going on as I did—public seminars, numerous books and interviews, and a Zen center to run that seemed to demand as much of his time as my businesses demanded of me.

I wanted to know how he did it—did he meditate every day? How long for? How did he structure the meditations? How long would it take me to get to the same level of peace that he seemed to have?

He seemed almost amused by the pace and intensity of my questions. Finally, he answered me like this:

"I do what I do, but I am no longer interested in attaining anything."

At first, that made our situations seem even more different, because there are still many things I hope to achieve and attain in my lifetime. But as I lay back and relaxed before drifting off to sleep that evening, suddenly it struck me!

My life was about *doing* as much as I could to *have* lots of things so I could *be* happy. The real difference between the way I lived my life and the way my friend was living his was in the order we were doing things. He was *being* at peace, *doing* what needed to be done, and still *having* many of the same things that I was working so hard to get to.

While I am not and will likely never be mistaken for a Zen master, I now spend even more time focused on *being* relaxed and simply *doing* what needs to be done each day. I have just as much on the outside, but it is now supported by a much stronger foundation on the inside.

Here's the key:

Once you are able to simply be, doing and having will flow naturally from that place.

As a result of making this transition, I would now say that one of the things that jumps out at me when I work with people is how difficult many of them find it to just be with themselves. If they sit still for even a few moments they get uncomfortable and have to do something to distract themselves from how they feel. Their entire lives are set up all day long to stop them from ever having to feel even a little bit of discomfort or unease.

Many people have this problem to some degree. Some people can't be with themselves when they look in the mirror, some when they are alone late at night. The irony is that if you are willing to be with yourself in the face of your discomfort, the uncomfortable feeling begins to change into something much more pleasant surprisingly quickly.

If you have begun doing the exercises in this book and using the hypnotic trance, then you have already begun the process of changing this in yourself. Each one of these things helps to recalibrate your emotional responses to the world, so that you experience more emotional equilibrium.

Every stressful emotion is like a signal from your mind telling you there's something to pay attention to in your world. Generally speaking, anger is telling you to take action, fear to keep alert, and sadness to take time out to nurture yourself. When your emotions don't need to shout so loudly to be heard, you begin to experience more of the good feelings that are there in the background most of the time.

The 80/20 Rule

One of the most difficult things about making the change from "Do-Have-Be" to "Be-Do-Have" was creating space in my life to just be. I had been so successful at filling up every moment of my time with people and activities that there was almost no time left for me.

One question that really helped me to reprioritize came from a speech given by Steve Jobs, founder of Apple computers and one of the true geniuses of our time. When he was told that he might be dying of a rare form of cancer, he began to ask himself this question:

**If today were the last day of my life, would I
want to do what I am about to do today?**

It was at around that time that one of my friends had to change mobile phones and get a new number. Before giving the new number out to people, he decided to try a little experiment.

He had already successfully used something called the 80/20 rule to restructure his business, so he decided to see if it would make the same kind of positive difference in his life.

The 80/20 rule was first put forward by Wilfred Pareto, a 19th-century economist who was surprised to discover that 80 percent of the world's wealth was concentrated in the hands of only 20 percent of the world's population. What was even more remarkable to him was that this

80/20 divide seemed to hold true in nearly every area of life.

Check to see how many of these 80/20 patterns are true for you:

- *80 percent of your time is spent on 20 percent of your problems*

- *80 percent of your results come from 20 percent of your efforts*

- *80 percent of the wear on your carpets takes place on 20 percent of the area*

- *80 percent of the time you wear 20 percent of your clothes*

My friend made the assumption that 80 percent of his stress was probably coming from about 20 percent of the people he knew, so he made a list of everyone in his life who took his energy up and all the people who brought his energy down. And then he didn't give the new number to the ones he no longer wanted to spend time with!

Here is a version of this same 80/20 exercise you can use for yourself. As you take the time to complete your energy audit and review your answers, chances are that you will find a number of simple changes you can make that will allow you more time to just be happy without having to give up any of the activities, people, or things that make a positive difference in your life . . .

THE ENERGY AUDIT

1. Do an "80/20 audit" on the people, activities, and situations in your life. Ask yourself these questions now:

    •   What are the 20 percent of your activities that bring you 80 percent of your results?

    •   What are the 20 percent of your activities and areas of your life in which you experience 80 percent of your stress?

    •   What are the 20 percent of your activities and areas of your life in which you experience 80 percent of your happiness?

    •   Who are the 20 percent of the people in your life with whom you have 80 percent of your best experiences?

    •   Who or what brings your energy up when you think about them? Who or what brings your energy down?

2. Based on what you've learned, what should you be doing less of? What would be worth doing more of?

3. Who would it be worth spending more time with? Who would it be worth spending less time with?

4. If you had only one month to live, what would you let go of from your life? Which of those things can you let go of anyway?

CHAPTER TWELVE

•

The Secret of Joy

A Laughing Matter

> "The only true measure of success is the amount of joy we are feeling."
>
> ABRAHAM–HICKS

There is now a growing movement of doctors who make a medical case for daily laughter as a practical tool for better health and quality of life. One in particular, Dr. Madan Kataria, is a pioneer of Laughter Yoga. His research has shown that laughing for 15 to 20 minutes a day, even if the laughter is for no reason, increases the levels in your body of specific neurotransmitters known as "endorphins."

Endorphins are your body's natural opiates, and their presence in your body can reduce pain, alleviate symptoms of bronchitis and asthma, and even increase stamina in athletes. Dr. Kataria's "laughter clubs" have become popular around the world. Ironically, there are more laughter clubs in Germany than anywhere else in the world!

Having a sense of humor is a vital psychological resource, not just because laughter releases positive chemicals into the body but also because in order to find something funny, we have to be able to see it from multiple perspectives.

When someone is experiencing higher than usual levels of stress, their focus tends to become blinkered as they focus in more and more exclusively on the problem or difficulty they are facing. This temporary inability to shift perspectives is what results in the loss of their sense of humor.

But the fact is that whether they are stressed or not, many people have been conditioned out of being spontaneously humorous. They have been taught that their serious faces show the world how intelligent they are, and they believe that laughter is somehow incompatible with being respected or taken seriously.

For example, whenever I do a corporate training, I always ask the executives to show me their biggest smiles. Many of them look as though their faces are going to crack. When they do finally allow themselves to laugh, it is as though someone has taken ten years off their faces. Their shoulders relax, they breathe more deeply, and often they find answers to questions and solutions for problems that have been stumping them for weeks.

The point is, humor is one of your most valuable resources in the effort to control your stress, so it's helpful to find opportunities to laugh every single day. You can do this by watching or listening to comedy, laughing for no reason, or simply by finding a more humorous perspective on things at appropriate times in your everyday life.

Remember, every time you laugh, you stimulate the release of chemicals in the brain that enhance your well-being. Even if you only stop to remember times from the past when you have laughed, particularly when you laughed long and hard, you produce a flood of good feelings in your body that will stop the stress response in its tracks.

Background happiness

If you are drowning in a sea of inescapable stress, every little thing that happens tends to seem worse than it really is. But when you are floating comfortably on a sea of good feelings, any little waves in the ocean won't really affect you. You will still notice them, of course, and take any appropriate action to handle them, but your world won't be rocked every time there's a bump in the road.

Background happiness is a subtle but all-pervading awareness that regardless of what is going on around you, all is well. It is characterized by a state of relaxed alertness with good feelings in your body and positive thoughts in your mind.

Many people already create this sense of optimism in their lives simply by focusing on the many things we all have in our lives to feel good about.

In one fascinating study "happiness psychologist" Dr. Robert Holden showed that if a group of depressed people regularly think about things that make them feel good, their brain chemistry changes so much that they can no longer stay depressed.

He asked them to laugh (or simulate laughter) for 20 minutes a day and do some physical exercise every day. They were also taught to think positive thoughts throughout the day in order to refocus their attention on the positive.

In less than a month, they had reprogrammed their brains to produce powerful positive feelings *regardless of what was going on in their lives.* A scientific study into the group showed that they had moved from one end of the scale to the other—from being clinically depressed to being happy optimists.

Further studies showed that six months afterwards the structure of their physical brains had actually been changed through the process. In a sense, happiness had become hardwired into the system.

Similarly, when I was writing *I Can Make You Rich*, I asked people everywhere I went and from every socioeconomic group what they would change in their lives if they had significantly more money. Remarkably, even the financially poorest among them wouldn't change that much. While they might want to upgrade their home, car, or clothes, the vast majority of people wouldn't change their profession, the things they laugh at or their friends.

Whether or not you feel this is true of you as well, the fact is that *we don't ever need a reason to feel good.* Happy feelings are just neurochemical events, so if we could just learn to control our body chemistry, we could summon up the right mix of thoughts and feelings to create a cocktail of electrochemical happiness.

Well, the good news is we can! As you have been discovering throughout this book, the more you learn to relax in any moment, the easier it will be to experience a general sense of relaxed alertness and well-being throughout the day.

Bliss on Demand

One evening, I was working on developing a new technique for summoning good feelings quickly. I spent almost 20 minutes vividly remembering a number of times I had enjoyed a massive endorphin release in the past—winning an award, laughing hard with my friends, slipping into a warm bath at the end of the day, and several things that I would blush to mention!

After associating myself back into these experiences over and over again in my mind, my body was flooded with endorphins. I then created an anchor for this blissful state by linking those feelings to the squeeze of the thumb and index finger on my right hand. I kept remembering the good times over and over again while squeezing my thumb and finger together until the link was firmly established. I had created an "endorphin release button"—all I had to do was give it a squeeze and my brain knew exactly what to do to give me a release of endorphins.

Now, as it happened I was hungry, so I decided to go out and pick up a pizza while still "high" on my own brain chemistry. The dour-looking teenager behind the counter just stared at me as I approached the counter.

"What are you so happy about?" he growled.

With a smile, I replied, "Absolutely nothing!"

About a month later, I demonstrated this technique at a talk I was giving to a group of health-care professionals. I received a wonderful letter from a psychiatrist who attended that evening who began using the "endorphin button" technique with depressed patients, with great success.

Of course, you don't have to be depressed to use this technique—in fact, the more you use it, the more likely you will begin to experience background happiness in your life.

Here's how you can create this "button" for yourself:

THE ENDORPHIN BUTTON

1. Remember a time you had a release of endorphins: making love, laughing, or another moment of euphoria when your body tingled with pleasure.

2. Vividly return to that time like you are back there again now, see what you saw, hear what you heard, and feel how good you felt.

3. As you recall this memory, make the colors in the memory brighter, the sounds louder.

4. Now squeeze the thumb and index finger together on your right hand as you recall the memory five times in a row.

5. When you only have to squeeze your thumb and index finger and recall the memory for the endorphin feeling to flood back, you have created an endorphin switch.

Each time you do this exercise, you will find it easier to relax, let go, and laugh at many of the things in your life that used to bother you. This does not mean you are no longer concerned about them—just that by being willing to take them (and yourself) a little bit more lightly, you will find better solutions when you need to and find it easier to let go when you don't.

•

CHAPTER THIRTEEN

The Power of Appreciation

How to Increase Your Joy!

> "Gratitude is not only the greatest of virtues, but the parent of all the others."
>
> CICERO

Far too many people, particularly when they are stressed, spend all of their time thinking about everything that is wrong or could go wrong in their lives. To return to the earlier metaphor of stress as a car alarm, instead of being the car, people have become the alarm.

One of the most basic facts of human psychology is this:

What we practice, we get good at.

When people have been in stress for a long time, they've been overly concerned with what's not working and with what's gone wrong. They've trained themselves to focus on problems in an attempt to prevent them from happening. Like the news, which tends to seek out the most negative story from all the possible things that could be reported, they've become specialists in "disaster awareness."

We all know that the more you use a muscle, the stronger it gets. In the same way, every time you think about something in a certain way, your brain fires specific electrical impulses down specific neural pathways. The more times those electrical impulses are fired down the same pathways, the stronger and more developed those pathways become.

When people are constantly thinking about everything that could go wrong, it is as though they are "practicing" being in a state of high alert. Each one of these practice sessions reinforces the neural networks in their brains associated with fear and stress, so it actually becomes easier for them to go into the stress response than to experience feelings of happiness and joy.

One of the best ways to change this is to begin to shift the primary orientation of your thinking from "what's wrong" to "what's right." This is not like positive thinking, which says you shouldn't ever look at the downside or feel an uncomfortable feeling. It's simply a process of retraining your brain to begin to notice more and more of the joy and wonder that surround us in any moment.

In the same way as people have habituated to focus on what's missing from their lives, you can train your brain over a period of days to notice everything that's joyous and wonderful. The two techniques in this chapter have been thoroughly and scientifically tested, and the results are clear.

What you focus on consistently, you get more of.

What we will be doing in this next exercise is building a complimentary set of neural pathways so that your brain will begin to default to feelings of natural joy and relaxation. As you continually instruct your brain to pay attention to good feelings, it will notice them more and more often.

The more you notice when you already feel good, the more your brain will seek out additional good feelings—it's like buying a particular car and suddenly seeing that car everywhere. What you set your brain up to look for, it will begin to find.

At the beginning of this book, I asked you to put your hand on your heart and focus on positive feelings to help you control your stress and shift into a better feeling state. Now, we are going to use that same anchor in reverse to create more joy . . .

I FEEL GOOD

1. From this moment forward, any time you notice yourself feeling a particularly good feeling in your body, put your hand on your heart and take a moment to acknowledge how good it feels.

2. Give your mind the instruction to seek out more of this good feeling in the future or simply say out loud "I feel good" (or "happy," or whatever good feeling you are feeling in that moment).

Simple as it seems, doing this throughout the day for a period of as little as seven days will make a dramatic difference in the quality of your experience and your overall sense of joy and well-being.

The Sunset in Auschwitz

The famous psychiatrist Viktor Frankl was a survivor of the concentration camps during World War II. He went on to write one of the seminal books about that time, called *Man's Search for Meaning.*

When I first read the book, I expected it to be filled with horror stories about the brutalities of the Nazis, and it was. But to my surprise, much of what he wrote pointed to a simple but powerful truth: that even in the most horrific, horrendous environment, we can still have the direct experience of joy.

The story that stands out in my mind was his description of a group of prisoners at the end of a brutal day in the camp being captivated by the beauty of a sunset.

Whenever I am feeling a bit overwhelmed by my circumstances, I try to remind myself that joy and beauty are always present, all around us—and the more you train your brain to spot them, the more joy you will begin to experience in your own life.

An Attitude of Gratitude

Perhaps the most powerful tool in our attempt to reboot our natural joy system is also the simplest—making a daily list of all the things that we appreciate, that we are grateful for, or that bring us joy.

This list can include both big and small things—absolutely anything you appreciate and/or are grateful for in your life.

For example:

- Thinking about my family.

- The first cup of coffee in the morning.

- Winning an award.

- Hitting a fantastic golf shot.

- Hearing my favorite song come on the radio.

The benefits of this simple exercise are dramatic, including fewer physical symptoms, greater optimism, higher goal achievement, and increased levels of the positive states of alertness, enthusiasm, determination, attentiveness, and energy.

THE JOY LIST

1. Get a notebook or open a file on your computer where you can begin keeping track of the many experiences of joy and gratitude you experience throughout the day.

2. Each day, add at least five things to the list.

    Any time you are feeling in need of a boost, take the time to read back through what you have written—your levels of gratitude, appreciation, and joy will rise, taking your feelings back up to a higher level of consciousness.

When we focus on our appreciation, gratitude, and joy, we are celebrating our own abundance and creativity. Instead of habituating to the good things in our lives, making a joy list wakes us up to the simple pleasures of a life well lived.

CHAPTER FOURTEEN

•

Frequently
Asked Questions

Q. I have too much going on at the same time. I feel I'm constantly juggling too many plates, which means I end up not finishing anything—how can I cope?

First, you need to prioritize. A number of years ago I suddenly had a significant shift in my life success. This brought me more stress than ever before—I was overwhelmed by the number of possibilities and things to do. So I started every day by looking at what was on the "To Do" list and giving each task an A, B, or C.

> *A = Urgent and must be done ASAP.*
>
> *B = Important, but can wait.*
>
> *C = Everything else.*

My stress levels dropped immediately, knowing that I would work my way through the As, then the Bs, and if I had some time left I'd get around to the Cs.

When you use this simple system for yourself, you will find that nothing important gets missed or falls through the cracks—the worst thing that ever happens is a few lower-priority tasks have to wait a day or two to get done.

Q. I don't see how I can set aside recovery time for myself when I have so much to do.

Actually, you can't afford not to. It's a false economy to think that by just working harder and longer you're going to get more done.

Imagine what would happen to athletes who trained 18 hours a day and didn't take the time to rest, recover, or eat healthy foods—they would collapse within a short period of time and become completely unable to perform.

The truth is, when you have no recovery time you burn out faster.

Ask yourself: what will be the cost of carrying on the way you are now over the next six months?

The next year?

The next five years?

Simply taking a bit of time each day to relax deeply and exercise your body is enough to get started. Over time, you will find you have become so much more efficient and effective in managing your energy that you can afford to take even more time off without diminishing the amount you are able to achieve.

Q. I end up taking on too much and agree-ing to stuff I don't want to do because I don't like disappointing people—how can I learn to say no?

As with any other nonproductive behavior, agreeing to too much has a positive intention, which is gener-ally to make more of a difference or be of greater service to others.

The irony is that in your effort to please as many people as possible, you end up disappointing them all, because you can only do so much and you end up doing everything only half as well. You are far better off doing fewer things, but doing them to the best of your ability.

When you actually stop and imagine how bad it's going to be to disappoint the people whose opinion you value, it will give you the motivation to start to priori-tize. Ask yourself, "If I could only get one thing done today, what would it be?"

Do that one thing as if it was the only thing you had to do today. When it's complete, go back, ask yourself the question again and repeat the process.

What I now say to people when I recognize that I have too much on my plate is simply this:

"I would love to help, but I am overwhelmed at the moment and I am sure you will understand that I don't want to let you down. I will let you know when I am able to do it."

Q. I always want things to be perfect, which means I end up spending too much time on tasks that others seem to find relatively simple. Why can't I just get on and do things?

I once heard the story of a Zen monk who was very eager to impress an important visitor to his monastery. He worked tirelessly for days to create the perfect Zen garden. Every tree was trimmed just so and every waterfall, stone, and pebble was carefully placed.

When the visitor arrived, he looked around with a bemused expression on his face. He then walked over to the largest tree in the garden and shook it until half a dozen leaves had fallen to the ground in a random pattern. He smiled at the monk.

"Now," he said, "it is perfect!"

Being a perfectionist has a positive intention—however, when it's taken to an extreme it drives you and everyone else around you crazy. (I've even seen some perfectionists try to be perfectly imperfect!)

Trying to get everything "just so" can become an obsession, and like any habit, the more you feed it the stronger it gets. So you need to decide you are going to allow some things not to be quite perfect.

For example, in theory you could create an orchestra where all the instruments were played by a computer. Every note would be absolutely perfect, but it would have no soul. What actually brings the music to life are the tiny imperfections.

Q. I get panic attacks when I'm stressed but I really don't want to take medication for it. Can your techniques help with this?

Yes, the techniques in this book can and will help, and the hypnotic trance will almost certainly make a positive difference. However, it may well be best to seek professional help.

Panic attacks are simply your mind and body over-signaling emotionally in an attempt to get your attention. When someone ignores an emotional signal, the emotion gets stronger and stronger. If the message behind the emotion continues unheeded for long enough, it can become a full-blown panic attack.

Even though the original cause for concern may no longer be present, the emotional signal carries on, like an alarm that keeps on ringing long after the emergency has passed.

As you reestablish your emotional equilibrium, your overall levels of fear and anxiety will decrease and you will experience more and more positive feelings throughout the day.

FOURTEEN-DAY

Gratitude Journal

YOUR JOURNAL

> "Keeping a journal will absolutely change your life in ways you've never imagined."
>
> OPRAH WINFREY

If you've never kept a journal before, prepare to be amazed at the difference it will make in your life. The act of writing down what you appreciate and what you enjoy trains your brain to make gratitude and joy your natural emotional default position.

As you focus on these positive thoughts, you are building neural networks in your brain associated with feelings of joy and well-being. This will make it easier and easier for you to automatically think in this way. As I explained earlier, scientific experiments show that by repeatedly thinking about things that make you feel good, you alter your brain chemistry for the better. You can and will literally "hardwire" yourself to feeling good more and more of the time throughout the day.

May your dearest wishes come true!

God bless you,
Paul McKenna

DAY 1

Today, I appreciate . . .

_____

_____

_____

Today, I am grateful for . . .

_____

_____

_____

My favorite moment of today was . . .

_____

_____

_____

DAY 2

Today, I appreciate . . .

_____

_____

_____

Today, I am grateful for . . .

_____

_____

_____

My favorite moment of today was . . .

_____

_____

_____

DAY 3

Today, I appreciate . . .

_____

_____

_____

Today, I am grateful for . . .

_____

_____

_____

My favorite moment of today was . . .

_____

_____

_____

DAY 4

Today, I appreciate . . .

_____

_____

_____

Today, I am grateful for . . .

_____

_____

_____

My favorite moment of today was . . .

_____

_____

_____

DAY 5

Today, I appreciate…

_____

_____

_____

Today, I am grateful for…

_____

_____

_____

My favorite moment of today was…

_____

_____

_____

DAY 6

Today, I appreciate...

_____

_____

_____

Today, I am grateful for...

_____

_____

_____

My favorite moment of today was...

_____

_____

_____

DAY 7

Today, I appreciate...

_____

_____

_____

Today, I am grateful for...

_____

_____

_____

My favorite moment of today was...

_____

_____

_____

DAY 8

Today, I appreciate…

_____

_____

_____

Today, I am grateful for…

_____

_____

_____

My favorite moment of today was…

_____

_____

_____

DAY 9

Today, I appreciate...

_____

_____

_____

Today, I am grateful for...

_____

_____

_____

My favorite moment of today was...

_____

_____

_____

DAY 10

Today, I appreciate...

_____

_____

_____

Today, I am grateful for...

_____

_____

_____

My favorite moment of today was...

_____

_____

_____

DAY 11

Today, I appreciate...

_____

_____

_____

Today, I am grateful for...

_____

_____

_____

My favorite moment of today was...

_____

_____

_____

DAY 12

Today, I appreciate...

_____

_____

_____

Today, I am grateful for...

_____

_____

_____

My favorite moment of today was...

_____

_____

_____

DAY 13

Today, I appreciate...

_____

_____

_____

Today, I am grateful for...

_____

_____

_____

My favorite moment of today was...

_____

_____

_____

GRATITUDE JOURNAL • 145

DAY 14

Today, I appreciate...

_____

_____

_____

Today, I am grateful for...

_____

_____

_____

My favorite moment of today was...

_____

_____

_____

A FINAL WORD

By now, you have probably begun to notice some changes. Perhaps you are feeling more relaxed—less worried, with an almost inexplicable sense of ease and well-being.

The more you use the techniques in this book and listen to the hypnotic trance, the better your life will get. The better your life gets, the better it is for everyone around you.

One of the major problems facing the world today is too much stress, anxiety, and worry, and not enough relaxed, happy joy. I truly believe that if we could all just relax a bit more as a planet, then many of our problems would clear up.

May you be blessed—all is well!

Until we meet,
Paul McKenna

We hope you enjoyed this Hay House book. If you'd like to receive our online catalog featuring additional information on Hay House books and products, or if you'd like to find out more about the Hay Foundation, please contact:

Hay House, Inc., P.O. Box 5100, Carlsbad, CA 92018-5100
(760) 431-7695 or (800) 654-5126
(760) 431-6948 (fax) or (800) 650-5115 (fax)
www.hayhouse.com® • www.hayfoundation.org

• • •

Published and distributed in Australia by:
Hay House Australia Pty. Ltd., 18/36 Ralph St., Alexandria NSW 2015
Phone: 612-9669-4299 • *Fax:* 612-9669-4144 • www.hayhouse.com.au

Published and distributed in the United Kingdom by:
Hay House UK, Ltd., Astley House, 33 Notting Hill Gate, London W11 3JQ
Phone: 44-20-3675-2450 • *Fax:* 44-20-3675-2451 • www.hayhouse.co.uk

Published and distributed in the Republic of South Africa by:
Hay House SA (Pty), Ltd., P.O. Box 990, Witkoppen 2068
info@hayhouse.co.za • www.hayhouse.co.za

Published in India by: Hay House Publishers India,
Muskaan Complex, Plot No. 3, B-2, Vasant Kunj, New Delhi 110 070
Phone: 91-11-4176-1620 • *Fax:* 91-11-4176-1630 • www.hayhouse.co.in

Distributed in Canada by:
Raincoast Books, 2440 Viking Way, Richmond, B.C. V6V 1N2
Phone: 1-800-663-5714 • *Fax:* 1-800-565-3770 • www.raincoast.com

• • •

Take Your Soul on a Vacation

Visit www.HealYourLife.com® to regroup, recharge, and reconnect with your own magnificence. Featuring blogs, mind-body-spirit news, and life-changing wisdom from Louise Hay and friends.

Visit www.HealYourLife.com today!

Paul McKenna, Ph.D., is described by Ryan Seacrest as "a cross between the Dr. Phil and Tony Robbins of Britain." Recently named by the *London Times* as one of the world's leading and most important modern gurus, alongside Nelson Mandela and the Dalai Lama, he is Britain's best-selling nonfiction author, selling 8,000 books a week in 35 countries—a total of 8 million books in the last decade. He has worked his unique brand of personal transformation with Hollywood movie stars, Olympic gold medalists, rock stars, leading business achievers, and royalty. Over the past 20 years, Paul McKenna has helped millions of people successfully quit smoking, lose weight, overcome insomnia, eliminate stress, and increase self-confidence. Dr. McKenna has appeared on *The Dr. Oz Show, Good Morning America, The Ellen DeGeneres Show, Rachael Ray, Anderson Live,* and *The Early Show.* He is regularly watched on TV by hundreds of millions of people in 42 countries around the world.

Dr. McKenna has consistently astounded his audiences and clients by proving how small changes in people's lives can yield huge results, whether it's curing someone of a lifelong phobia or clearing up deep-seated issues in a matter of minutes. He currently hosts his own TV show on Hulu, where he interviews the most interesting people in the world. His guests include Simon Cowell, Harvey Weinstein, Rachael Ray, Sir Roger Moore, Roger Daltrey, Tony Robbins, Paul Oakenfold, and Sir Ken Robinson. Website: www.mckenna.com

**FOR MORE INFORMATION
GO TO
mckenna.com**